SIGMUND FREUD

MAKERS OF MODERN THOUGHT

EDITOR:

THE REV. DR. A. D. GALLOWAY

PROFESSOR OF DIVINITY, UNIVERSITY OF GLASGOW

CONSULTANT EDITORS: The Rev. Joseph D. Ban (Chaplain, Linfield College, McMinnville, Oregon, U.S.A.), the Rev. Alec Gilmore (Associate Editor, Lutterworth Press), and the Rev. Frank Hoadley (Editor, Judson Press, U.S.A.)

SIGMUND FREUD

by

MICHAEL HARE DUKE
Bishop of St. Andrews

JUDSON PRESS
VALLEY FORGE, PENNSYLVANIA 19481

International Standard Book No. 0–8170–0558–7
Library of Congress Catalog Card No. 76–182460
Copyright © 1972 Lutterworth Press

Judson Press Edition 1972

Printed in Great Britain

CONTENTS

INTRODUCTION

Behind the Concious Mind

SIGMUND FREUD is one of those few pioneers whose discoveries have altered the whole texture of our thinking about human behaviour. Although relatively few people would be capable of giving any coherent statement of what he actually said, the effects of his conclusions are woven into all sorts of assumptions that form part of our background thinking.

When we watch a television play and accept the author's assumption that his hero's strange behaviour might be linked to some inner, unrecognized need, then we are acknowledging ourselves members of a post-Freudian thought-world. If we feel that the behaviour of a delinquent may have something to do with his upbringing and that he steals now because once he was deprived of love, then we are using a model for understanding human behaviour that derives from Vienna.

Perhaps it will be easiest to make the point from a more detailed example. A patient described a dream that he had had to his therapist. He had been, he said, in a shop that reminded him of an old fashioned ironmonger's. Lining the walls had been rows of boxes full of nails. Coming at him down an alley-way had been a steam engine designed rather like Stevenson's Rocket with a huge funnel. It had rolled towards him threatening to crush him until he had awakened with the fear of the nightmare. If a friend told one such a dream one might laugh it off as the effect of too good a dinner, or remember that something seen the night before on television was similar, and one could attribute it to that. Both these facts might be true and yet there remains the interesting question as to why of all the images that have been in front of the mind in the previous twenty-four hours these particular ones should have been selected? Directed towards a deeper inquiry the patient suggested that the setting of the dream had something to do with the fact that his father had owned an ironmonger's. What was his relationship with his father? He had felt dominated, crushed by him. Since the patient had come for help precisely because he felt that he was 'no proper man' it would appear that the dream was a significant communication about what he felt his father had done to him, but couched in picture language that could be told without the conscious guilt of making an accusation, even to the therapist, against his parent.

But if that were true, why could it not be stated straight out? Why was there a need to go about it by a devious route of dream interpretation? In his rational thought the patient revered his father's memory; he would not have felt it right to make so fundamental an accusation against him. It needed the picture language of the dream to allow the idea to 'escape' out of the unconscious mind and be accepted in consciousness. Such a piece of understanding comes directly from the explorations conducted by Freud. Although dreams have always fascinated the inquiring mind and have suggested ideas of supernatural communication, it was he who used them as 'the royal road' into the unconscious mind.

But then the notion of 'the unconscious mind' is also something which he pioneered. Through the generations men have always been aware of a conflict within themselves. St. Paul wrote, 'the good that I would I do not,

8

and that which I hate, that I do.' It was left to Freud to ask the question, 'What are the forces within a man's own self which seem to undermine his conscious resolve?' A person may, consciously, say that he wishes to go to work but he has an overwhelming fear that stops him. How is this to be explained? Even more difficult perhaps is the other problem where someone has the same desire to go to work but is prevented from this by a physical pain, or even a paralysis, for which the doctors can find no organic cause. What explanation is to be offered for this phenomenon? Freud would reply that something is going on in the personality of which the conscious mind is unaware. In this case there must be another centre of motivation which can only be called 'the unconscious mind'.

As a doctor Freud began his studies with sick patients but he quickly began to apply his theories to the general run of society; the same mechanisms were shown to operate in ordinary people as in his neurotic patients. So he explored what he described as 'the psychopathology of everyday life'. By this he meant that if it is reasonable to ask of a person where in their past the roots of their obviously delinquent or unacceptable behaviour lie, it must be perfectly possible to explore the more normal phenomena like the slips of the tongue or lapses of memory along the same lines of inquiry.

'How stupid, I forgot to bring any money out with me!' says a woman in the supermarket. Is it fair to wonder whether, although this person said she was going on a shopping expedition, part of her felt fairly deeply against the enterprise and so made certain that it would be frustrated by leaving behind the necessary ingredient, the money?

Is there something significant in our relationship with a person whose name we consistently forget? Or what

9

about a stammer? In many cases this seems to be a physical expression of an attempt to communicate and an attempt to stop communication going on at the same time. The conscious will of the person is clearly to talk; where does the opposition come from? All these inquiries seem to point to the same fact that even the ordinary person has got a part of himself of which he is unaware. Nowadays we more or less take this insight for granted. It was Freud who first pointed it out, but his inquiries did not stop when he had uncovered the unrecognized conflict in the present. He was convinced that this was a first step right back into the beginnings of the personality.

As soon as one admits that unconscious motives can be at work in anyone, then it seems as though the whole careful structure of rational thought is endangered. What can be trusted any more? To go back to our example of the dream about the steam roller in the ironmonger's shop: in its present form this is reported by the therapist who worked with the patient. How can we be sure that the report is accurate and not subject to the distortion of unconscious needs in the reporter? Suppose he was some-one who wrestled with unrecognized conflicts about his relations with his father, might not he impart into the interpretation not objective criteria but his own person-ality needs?

It is a curious paradox that psycho-analytical methods can seem to be both the guardians of rationality and the most dangerous way of undermining rational argument. It may be claimed that the purpose of the inquiry which is undertaken is to eliminate the irrational elements in any thinking process and leave only the true perceptions of fact and valid conclusions. The difficulty comes in practice when two people who are engaged in argument have got to agree what is objective truth and what is subjective distortion. A typical exchange might go: 'That is how things are: I wonder why you see them so differently.' 'What is it in you that always has to evade facing the truth?' On that basis it could go on *ad infinitum.*

It is part of the cost of living in a post-Freudian age that wherever anyone makes a statement it is always possible for his opponent to question not his facts or his logical premisses but his personality.

It may be that in this lies one of the reasons for a great deal of hostility directed against too deep an inquiry into human behaviour. There is no doubt that Freud and his followers have been the objects of direct attack and also continuous misrepresentation. It is hoped that the brief exposition of what he actually taught may help a little towards a more valid estimation by the next generation. At the same time we must try to make some sort of estimate of how far Freud was himself the prisoner of his past and the cultural climate in which his research was undertaken. In spite of his own rigorously conducted self-analysis, how far did he rid himself of his prejudices so that, for instance, he saw the male-female relationship clearly? Given a different background and another set of experiences, might he have continued to think as he did about religious belief? Indeed how far is one doing justice to Freud's achievement if one does not use the psychiatrist's own insights for a refinement of his conclusions and an evaluation of them?

It is with these questions in mind that in the following chapters we shall first give a summary of the way that Freud's thought developed in the light of growing clinical experience and then seek to sum up his conclusions in the light of our present situation, more than fifty years after his main writings were first published.

I

LIFE

Early Influence

IT WAS IN THE YEAR 1873 that Sigmund Freud
enrolled at the University in Vienna as a medical
student. He was seventeen years old and had lived in
the city since his parents moved there from Freiberg
when he was three.

His background was undistinguished. His father, a
Jewish wool-merchant, was never a great commercial
success. The move from Freiberg was dictated by business
difficulties but it did not resolve them. Money was short
all through Freud's childhood and on into the early
years of his adult life. This fact, however, did not prevent
his father from seeing that his son Sigmund had an
education which matched his academic ability. So he
went to the Gymnasium in Vienna at which he had won
a place a year early, when he was nine, and where he
managed to spend most of his school life at the top of the
class.

But if the external events of Freud's early years were
uneventful his inner life was a complex web of relationships. When he was born, his father aged forty was at
the beginning of his marriage to a second wife twenty
years younger than himself. By his first marriage there
had been two sons, both now grown up and one of

them the father of a boy, John, whose companionship with his year-junior uncle became an important part of the early years.

In the second marriage, the boy Sigmund was followed by seven brothers and sisters. The first of these, Julius, died in infancy before Freud was two. In the three-volume biography written by Ernest Jones, a disciple of Freud and a fellow psycho-analyst, the comment appears: 'It is reasonable to suppose that (his) ruthless search into the meaning of humanity and human relations was first generated in connection with the puzzling problems of his early family life.'

As Freud's career advanced and his own personality developed, he became increasingly aware of the importance of the early years. In the course of his self-analysis, which he began intensively in the year 1897, he unravelled many of the tangled threads of the past, but all that belongs to a later part of the story. In 1873 the young Jewish student was simply an able boy who had decided rather half-heartedly on the career of medicine as being a preferable alternative to business or the law.

He certainly had no driving urge to plunge into the world of healing. Looking back he himself commented:

'After forty-one years of medical activity, my self-knowledge tells me that I have never been a doctor in the proper sense. I became a doctor through being compelled to deviate from my original purpose; and the triumph of my life lies in my having, after a long and roundabout journey, found my way back to my earliest path. I have no knowledge of having had in my early years any craving to help suffering humanity . . . In my youth I felt an overpowering need to understand something of the riddles of the world in which we live and perhaps even contribute something to their solution. The most hopeful means of achieving this end seemed to be to enrol myself in the medical faculty' (From the post-script to *The Question of Lay Analysis.*)

This attitude explains the leisurely progress of his academic career. Even the financial pressures of his family did nothing to urge him towards establishing a solid earning capacity.

Early Career

The Viennese medical school, although it provided the necessary course through which any clinician had to pass, was in fact without any practical involvement with patients and provided a useful field of study in the natural sciences. So Freud settled down to twenty-eight hours of lectures a week in botany, chemistry, micro-scopy, mineralogy, as well as the more obvious study of anatomy. In addition, he enrolled for a course on 'Biology and Darwinism'.

As he pursued these interests he found himself encouraged by the Professor of the Zoology Department to undertake research on the reproductive process in eels. This piece of work, which involved him in the dissection of more than 400 specimens, brought him to the end of his third year. At this point he began work in the Physiology Laboratory. Of the six years that he spent there he wrote, 'I found rest and satisfaction—and men too whom I could respect and take as my models' (Auto-biography 15). Here, under the influence of the Pro-fessor, Ernst Brücke, Freud learned an attitude to his research which was more than a disciplined use of the microscope; it was in effect a philosophy of life. For the school which Brücke followed believed that all human behaviour could be understood in terms of physical physiology. There was no room for a faith in ideals which drew you on; what a man was could be totally explained by the physical make-up of the organism. Such a belief presupposed that one was a radical materialist and also accepted the proposition that every event had an antecedent cause to explain it.

This point of view was part of the rational tradition of western thought stemming from Rousseau, Voltaire and the philosophers of the Enlightenment, but it had been recently challenged by a school of *Naturphilosophie* in Germany. This was a quasi-mystical view of nature which endeavoured in a system of 'speculative physics' to explain the world in terms of its ultimate purposes rather than by an exact study of its predisposing causes. It suggested that the world might be understood in terms of what it was meant to be, not by examining the facts of the past and present. At first sight, some of the language of Psycho-analysis, dealing as it does with ideas of 'purpose', 'intention' and 'aim', might seem to have moved away from the rigorous determinism of Brücke. In fact, Freud was always concerned to explain the origin of phenomena; if he was aware of a drive in man he wanted to know where it came from. So he remained true to his initial orientation. His purpose was to make sense of life and dispense with illusion, one aspect of which was religious belief. He himself summed it up, 'My life has been aimed at one goal only: to infer or to guess how the mental apparatus is constructed and what forces interplay and counteract in it.' (Jones, Vol. I, p. 49)

In 1881 Freud had been at the University for eight years and it became clear that although his bent was towards research there was no way in which he could hope to make an adequate living by continuing in his present sphere of activity. Freud described the moment of decision in his Autobiography: 'I took no interest in anything to do with medicine till the teacher whom I so deeply respected (Brücke) warned me that in view of my restricted material circumstances I could not possibly take up a theoretical career.' The restricted material circumstances included not only the poverty of his family but the fact that he was getting more and more deeply into debt with a number of his friends. Hard financial reality therefore demanded that Freud take his final examinations and find medical work.

The Emotions of Courtship

Freud took his M.D. in March 1881 but remained in the Institute of Physiology as a demonstrator for a further fifteen months. What finally made him take practical steps to embark on a career was the fact that he fell in love. The girl who achieved this profound revolution in him was a young Jewess, Martha Bernays, five years his junior. Their courtship and engagement was fraught with financial worries as to when it would ever be possible to think of getting married and also with emotional storms originating with Freud. When this reserved, scientifically-minded man came to the point of risking his love for another person he proved, as one might have predicted, possessive and jealous. It was not only potential rivals who were the object of suspicion but also her mother, her brother and her religious faith.

The engagement lasted for four years and most of this period was one of separation. As the couple wrote to one another nearly every day, a voluminous correspondence, carefully preserved, has served to chart the course of this often stormy period. In the light of the future it is interesting to notice how even at this stage his judgement in emotional matters can go beneath the surface appearance. Commenting on the difference of relationship that existed between Martha and her sister Minna and their mother, he wrote, 'You don't love her very much and are as considerate as possible to her : Minna loves her but doesn't spare her.'

It was during these years of courtship, 1882 to 1886, that vital changes took place in the direction of Freud's life. On seeking to find work as a doctor, he had taken a post at the Vienna General Hospital as a first step in acquiring clinical experience. With the aim of marriage in mind he began to try to work out various ways of establishing himself so that he could be assured of an income commensurate with his responsibilities. Although committed to the therapeutic field his mind naturally turned to the academic world of medicine, where his researches and published papers had given him a deserved reputation. He therefore set about seeking to become accredited as a *Privat Dozent*. This was a position within the University somewhat akin to a University lecturer and gave the holder the right to take pupils for a fee. Linked to this was a project for obtaining an award that would make it possible for him to travel to Paris and attend the lectures of the celebrated Professor Charcot at the Salpêtrière. By now it must have seemed clear to those who knew him that Freud's specialization was to lie in the field of neuropathology, and it was an obvious step forward to study under a doctor whose skill was internationally renowned. But what in fact emerged from the visit was not so much a question of neurology as a quite fresh insight arising from Charcot's dealing with the problem of hysteria.

This was the turning point which took Freud from his preoccupation with the physical aspect of the brain into his revolutionary study of the human mind.

2

THOUGHT

Hysteria

DOCTORS HAVE ALWAYS RECOGNIZED that from time to time they are faced with patients who are in genuine distress but for whose symptoms they can find no explanation in organic illness. These inexplicable manifestations had come to be lumped together under the diagnosis of hysteria, but when the doctor had given the illness a name it did not mean that he had any idea how to treat it. To say that a patient was suffering from hysteria was more a gesture of resignation than a positive step in the direction of therapy.

The traditional view had been that this was simply due to imagination, or else, following the ancient slander which derived the name of the disease from the Greek word *hystera* meaning 'womb', it was assumed to be a specifically feminine complaint and was associated with an irritation of the womb. Charcot in Paris made three important observations. First, he asserted that hysterical symptoms could be found in the male as well as the female. Secondly, he noted that the physical symptoms did not conform to the anatomy of the nervous system but affected a limb or part of the body as it appears to the external observation. Freud followed up this point and did research into the contrast between hysterical paralyses and those that were consequent upon damage to the nervous system. The conclusion was clear: 'Hysteria behaves as if anatomy did not exist or as though it had no knowledge of it.' Finally, by the use of hypnotism Charcot demonstrated that hysterical symptoms could be induced in those who were not hysterics, and sometimes symptoms which seemed to have arisen as the result of some specifically traumatic event could be removed by hypnotic suggestion.

These observations did not take Charcot as far as one might suppose in the understanding of illness. Having agreed to take it seriously, he then looked for a physiological cause, since this alone would make it a 'proper' disease. It was therefore his opinion that it was to be understood as connected with a deterioration of the brain which was an hereditary weakness. It was part of the originality of Freud to see the connection between the psychological factors in the presentation of the illness and its causation.

It seems that he may well have been helped to make this significant step by the experience of a Viennese doctor, Joseph Breuer, which had been confided to him some months before. Dr. Breuer had a patient who has become famous under the pseudonym of Anna O., whom he treated from December 1880 to June 1882. A highly intelligent girl of 21, she had developed a whole collection of symptoms in connection with the experience of nursing her father during his fatal illness. The two points of vital importance which emerged from a long and interesting case were that she discovered that when she could tell her doctor about the origin of a particular symptom, it immediately disappeared. From this experience she called it 'the talking cure'. The second, less obviously therapeutic, was that to Dr. Breuer's horror it became clear that this very attractive patient was not only violently in love with him but imagined him to be father of a phantasy child. Breuer took flight from such a situation, and it took a long time before the patient was cured and in fact became a distinguished innovator in the field of women's social work. Breuer, a close friend of Freud although fourteen years his senior, had confided the whole case history to him towards the end of 1882, so that this was already evidence which he had to add to Charcot's observations.

Returning from the expedition to Paris in 1886 Freud had a great many preoccupations in his personal and professional life. This was the year of his marriage and of his start in private practice. He was also engaged at a new neurological department in the Institute for Children's Diseases. Nevertheless he found time to pursue the ideas which he had absorbed from Charcot. He had offered to translate his third set of lectures into German but, more importantly, he was determined to pursue the ideas concerning hysteria.

An attempt to enthuse the medical world of Vienna with Charcot's views proved a disastrous failure. Freud felt himself ostracized and in retrospect seems to have even exaggerated the sense of being in opposition to the recognized medical authorities. However, his private practice was bringing him a considerable number of neurotic patients and he had to decide what methods of therapy he could conscientiously employ. For a short period he seems to have played safe and prescribed the more conventional remedies. Then at the end of 1887 he turned to hypnotic suggestion. While he was prepared to champion this method publicly, he did not find in practice that he was a very good hypnotist. In any case the method was unsatisfactory from two points of view; first, because it concentrated upon the symptom and did not deal with the underlying cause, and secondly, it involved an inherent contradiction; for while working with the patient the doctor was continually implanting the suggestions that the disorder did not exist, but the patient's presence in the consulting room was evidence that it did! With the memory of Breuer's success in getting behind the symptom to its cause, he wanted to inquire deeper. But when he did he became not only aware of a hidden agenda from the past but also in the present. He began to guess that sometimes, for instance, the patient accepted the doctor's suggestions in order to please him, so that when the contact was withdrawn the good effects ended as well. So there was an emotional transaction going on underneath the declared rational aim of achieving a cure.

The outcome of this period of experimentation was offered to the world for inspection in the publication of the famous *Studies in Hysteria* in which Breuer collaborated in 1895. This publication contained five case histories and chapters by both Breuer and Freud on the theory which underlay the illness and its treatment. By now, hypnosis was gradually slipping into the background and Freud was moving towards the discovery of the technique of 'free association'. The stages in the development were first the discovery that a patient could be urged towards a memory sometimes by questioning, sometimes by putting his hand on their forehead and applying pressure. This was still too directive and he finally became convinced that once any idea of censoriousness was relaxed, the patient would volunteer material which, however apparently irrelevant, could be discovered to have meaning.

This was the beginning of the technique of 'free association' which was to become, along with the interpretation of dreams, the chief way of bringing unconscious ideas into the area of the mind where they could be examined. The technique was for the patient normally lying relaxed on a couch to say whatever came into the mind and to let one idea flow into another without any attempt to control the train of thought. In this way 'associations' were made between ideas or symbols which the conscious mind kept carefully dissociated because of what their connection revealed. It was the work of the analyst to help the patient understand the meaning of some of the associations when they were not immediately apparent.

Here perhaps Freud's training in the physical disciplines of physiology was important. Offered the apparently meaningless meanderings of a patient, most physicians would have hurried the person on to something more obviously important. Because Freud was convinced that everything had a cause, he was prepared to listen patiently until the hidden sense in the communication emerged. Added to this, Freud had quite early become aware in his patients of an unwillingness to disclose memories that were painful or unwelcome and this he termed 'resistance'. It was not difficult to guess that perhaps the meaningless ideas might lead to the actual memory that was too unpleasant to express. This was to follow the same pattern of understanding that he had already applied to the symptoms of hysteria. Here he had come to the conclusion that rightly understood they led back to a painful trauma which had been repressed so that it was not directly accessible to observation.

Repression

Since the whole concept of repression and resistance is so fundamental to Freud's understanding it is perhaps best to use his own words to explain it. Lecturing in America in 1909 he put it this way: 'Let us suppose that in this lecture-room . . . there is someone who is causing a disturbance and whose ill-mannered laughter, chattering and shuffling with his feet are distracting my attention from my task. I have to announce that I cannot proceed with my lecture; and thereupon three or four of you who are strong men stand up and, after a short struggle, put the interrupter outside the door. So now he is "repressed" and I can continue my lecture. But in order that the interruption shall not be repeated, in case the individual who has been expelled should try to enter the room once more, the gentlemen who have put my will into effect place their chairs up against the door and thus establish a "resistance" after the repression has been accomplished. If you will now translate the two localities concerned into psychical terms as the "conscious" and the "unconscious" you will have before you a fairly good picture of the process of repression.'

In the course of the lecture Freud went on: 'At first sight it really seems impossible to trace a path from repression to the formation of symptoms. Instead of giving a complicated theoretical account, I will return here to the analogy which I employed earlier for my explanation of repression.

'If you come to think of it, the removal of the interrupter and the posting of the guardians at the door may not mean the end of the story. It may very well be that the individual who has been expelled and who has now become embittered and reckless, will cause us further trouble. It is true that he is no longer among us; we are free from his presence . . . But in some respects nevertheless the repression has been unsuccessful; for now he is making an intolerable exhibition of himself outside the room, and his shouting and banging on the door with his fists interfere with my lecture even more than his bad behaviour did before.

'In these circumstances we could not fail to be delighted if our respected president . . . should be willing to assume the role of mediator and peace-maker. He would have a talk with the unruly person outside and would then come to us with a request that he should be re-admitted after all; he himself would guarantee that the man would now behave better. On his authority we decide to lift the repression and peace and quiet are restored.

'This presents what is really no bad picture of the physician's task in the pycho-analytic treatment of the neuroses.' (*Five lectures on Psycho-Analysis. Lecture II*)

Put in such a form it all sounds very simple and it is easy to accept this kind of description of the way that painful, frightening or guilty thoughts or experiences are conveniently forgotten. There are plenty of examples from psychiatric sources to bear witness to the way that these repressed memories later take their toll of mental health; lying at the root of all the varieties of strange behaviour or irrational fears that can bar the way to rational living.

The essence of Freud's achievement was to see that such occurrences could be described in dynamic terms, as a process that was currently operative. This meant that with sufficient knowledge it was possible to intervene in order to change the outcome. It was the first step towards man's accepting responsibility for his inner life which before had seemed quite unpredictable, and had been seen only as a field for the operation of invasive demonic powers which at best might be controlled by ascetic practices or magical intervention. In this respect psycho-analysis was striking a blow for greater rationality in living.

The Phenomenon of 'Transference'

In the course of his painstaking work with the patients who came to him Freud had now reached a point at which he could claim to understand much more deeply the mechanisms by which communication was both achieved and thwarted. He had formulated the concepts of resistance and repression and he had also begun to understand the phenomenon of 'transference' by which powerful emotions, mostly of love or hate, which have built up in the past, are transferred to the therapist in the treatment situation. When this had happened to Breuer with Anna O. he had fled from the scene. Freud recounts how one patient emerging from hypnosis threw her arms round his neck. He continues the account: 'The unexpected entrance of a servant relieved us from a painful discussion . . . I was modest enough not to attribute the event to my own irresistible personal attraction and I felt that I had now grasped the nature of the mysterious element that was at work behind hypnotism.' (*Autobiography* p. 27.) That is to say, he recognized that it was more often the patient's feelings for the doctor which produced the good effects than the hypnosis.

In feeling like that, the patient was seeing the doctor as something more than his ordinary self. If these feelings could be understood by the patient in relation to his past history, then there was a chance to learn some fundamental truths about his inner self.

So the basic tools of psycho-analysis were formed. There followed the question of how to interpret the material which emerged from a patient when the techniques were brought into play.

Trauma

As Freud listened to the train of associations which

emerged, he found that his patients were apt to be led back to an experience in the very early years of their life usually between the ages of three and four when they had been traumatically seduced. So convincing did the evidence appear to be that he declared categorically that at the bottom of every case of hysteria would be found one or more premature sexual experiences. This communication was received with icy disbelief. But what sounded to his fellow doctors like a 'scientific fairy-tale' Freud was prepared to back up with eighteen detailed case histories.

What Freud had not yet come to appreciate was that there is a wide difference between the inner world where fantasy and fact are indistinguishable and the external sphere of history, where the only hard currency is in actual events. It must have been a moment of most unpalatable insight when the truth dawned upon him. Writing of it in 1914 Freud said: '. . . The result was at first helpless bewilderment. Analysis had led by the right paths back to these sexual traumas, and yet they were not true. Reality was lost from under one's feet. At that time I would gladly have given up the whole thing. . . . Perhaps I persevered only because I had no choice and could not then begin again at anything else. At last came the reflection that after all one has no right to despair because one has been deceived in one's expectations; one must revise them. If hysterics trace back their symptoms to fictitious traumas, this new fact signifies that they create such scenes in fantasy, and psychical reality requires to be taken into account alongside actual reality.'

When Freud was facing this crisis in the credibility of such a major part of his work, he was fortunately just beginning the totally new task of attempting a self-analysis. Working largely on his dreams, he doubtless was gaining a confidence in the validity of material which was emerging, and was also beginning to achieve a personal insight into the fact that sexuality is a feature of infancy as much as of puberty.

In the course of this self-analysis which he pursued over the years, Freud came to understand many features of his personality in the light of his childhood. He reflected upon the relationship with his brother's child John: 'Until the end of my third year we had been inseparable; we had loved each other and fought each other and, as I have already hinted, this childish relation has determined all my later feelings in my intercourse with persons of my own age. My nephew John has since then had many incarnations which have revivified first one and then another aspect of a character that is ineradicably fixed in my unconscious memory.' He goes on to add: 'An intimate friend and a hated enemy have always been indispensable to my emotional life.' And with that insight many things become clear about the way that important friendships first flourished and then failed in Freud's life.

But most important of all was the recovery of memories and emotions which elucidated the relationships with his parents. It might be generally acceptable to emphasize the contribution that a mother makes to the mental attitudes of her child: 'A man who has been the indisputable favourite of his mother keeps for life the feeling of a conqueror, that confidence of success often induces real success.' What was not nearly so easy to convey was that this kind of confidence was involved in what could only be called a sexual relation. In a letter which was written in the first year of the self-analysis, he recounts the memory of how he was stimulated by seeing his mother naked when he was somewhere between the ages of two and two and a half. It is in the same letter

28

that he reveals his awareness of the evil wishes that he had entertained aged 15 months against the newly-born brother who was less than a year his junior. When in fact the baby died aged only eight months there was the classical reaction of guilt, as though the ill-wishes had had a magically destructive effect.

By these means, within himself Freud was discovering the truth of infantile sexuality which was to be met with so much resistance by educated opinion at large and which has left behind the accusation that Freud reduced everything to sex.

Dreams

Freud himself thought that his two main contributions to human understanding were contained in his two works, *The Interpretation of Dreams* and the *Three Essays on the Theory of Sexuality,* both of which stem from this period of his development. It is important, therefore, to spend a considerable proportion of space in the elucidation of what he really meant in writing them.

Initially Freud felt that he had to argue a case for taking dreams seriously at all. They are regarded as confused and meaningless and so it is customary to dismiss them from memory quickly and completely. Against this prevailing attitude he argues: 'Not all dreams are alien to the dreamer, incomprehensible and confused. If you inspect the dreams of very young children, from eighteen months upwards, you will find them perfectly simple and easy to explain. Small children always dream of the fulfilment of wishes that were aroused in them the day before but not satisfied. You will need no interpretative art in order to find this simple solution; all you need to do is inquire into the child's experience on the previous day (the "dream day").'

Moving on from the experience of children, he still holds to the view that dreams basically are the expression of a wish. Why this does not appear to be the case with the dreams of adults is that the process has been subject to distortion. In sleep the conscious self is largely off duty; therefore it is a time when unconscious desires can be felt more powerfully. But if this material pushed its way into the dream in undisguised form, it would arouse so much anxiety that sleep would be disturbed. So there needs to be some form of censorship. This results in the manifest content of the dream that may be fleetingly recaptured on waking and which seems so chaotic a collection of symbols. It is in fact, he argues, the product of the 'dream-work' which has the latent dream thoughts to work on. This process of distortion is comparable to the way in which the symptoms of a neurotic illness are related to the underlying anxiety for which they supply a manageable outlet.

To unravel the meaning of the dream, it is not a matter of decoding a message where each symbol has an exact counterpart. As the dreamer takes each remembered aspect of the dream and associates round it, a variety of levels occur in the meaning. Some may relate to unacceptable hostile feelings that are part of the present, others may lead back to sexual frustrations of the distant past. It must be admitted that whenever dream interpretations are put down on paper they seem to have about them a quality of artificiality or even implausibility that is not true of the sense of living exploration which characterizes the process of dream analysis. This is because any account given as a case history is being presented to observers quite outside the analytical situation. What carries conviction at the time is the sense of recognition by the dreamer of a particular personal insight.

Nevertheless Freud thought that the only way of explaining his procedure was to give a number of examples of dream interpretation, drawn partly from his patients and partly from the insights achieved in his own self-analysis. Two of the most important features in the dream-work he called 'condensation' and 'displacement'; the best way to understand them is to see the process in action. There was an occasion when he had a dream which he recalled as being in two parts; all that he knew of the first half was a curious, imaginary word, 'Autodidasker'; the second was a picture of himself going to a colleague, Professor N., and saying, 'The patient about whose condition I consulted you recently is in fact only suffering from a neurosis, just as you suspected.' . . . It might not seem that there was much material there to work on, until it is appreciated that the economy of the dream work has crammed a whole collection of ideas into the single word 'Autodidasker'.

As Freud thought about it he began with the association of 'author'. (On the previous evening his wife had been reading a collection of stories by an Austrian writer, a friend of Freud's brother. She had commented on one where a man with great talents came to a bad end and had linked this with an expression of hopes and fears for their own children. This is important as the contents of the dream always take their start in the events of the previous day, the 'dream-day'.) From 'author' he went on to 'good upbringing' (the opposite of an 'auto-didact', a person who has taught himself): then 'Breslau'—a friend who had married had gone to live there: two men who lived in Breslau who had come to a bad end through women, Lasker and Lassalle: a novel of Zola's, *L'Oeuvre,* in which the author introduces himself with his name disguised into 'Sandoz' as a happily married character. Finally, there is the desire, in the second part of the dream, that Freud might be proved wrong in his fears.

Far more material is needed to make totally plausible to any reader the interpretation of the dream, but as the process of association unpacks the word 'Autodidasker', the meaning of condensation becomes clear. Secondly, it is to be noted that although Freud dreams about a patient this is by way of disguising his real concern for his children's future, using the technique of displacement to keep the anxious thoughts at bay.

The third feature of dream-work is not well illustrated by this example for mostly abstract thoughts and ideas are transposed into visual terms. Freud quotes two examples : a man dreams that he is an officer sitting at table opposite the Emperor, and this represents his opposition to his father; or a woman dreams that she is walking with two little girls whose ages differ by fifteen months and this gives the clue that two traumatic events of childhood that feature in the dream occurred fifteen months apart.

Finally, Freud examined the possibility that there might be a 'language' of dream that used symbols commonly recognizable without the lengthy research of association. He concluded that, largely in the sexual field, there were a regular collection of objects which had this function. Umbrellas, sticks, posts, trees, knives, daggers, pistols, taps and watering cans, all appear in his list of objects which represent the male genitals. Pits, cavities, boxes, snails, churches, equally represent the female genitals. If the reader knows Golding's novel, *The Spire*, it may be remembered how the author has used this kind of dream symbolism as one level of the drama. To read the book with Freud's ideas in mind gives a new clarity to many points in the story. Such an exercise might be one of the best ways of getting the 'feel' of the whole notion of dreams and their meanings.

Infantile Sexuality

The Interpretation of Dreams, published in 1899 had made clear Freud's growing understanding of the part that sexual feelings and needs play in the development of the personality from infancy onwards. His first full-scale exposition of this thesis was set out in *Three Essays on the Theory of Sexuality* published in 1905. The result was a storm of protest against this destructive attack on the innocence of childhood.

In fact, Freud was so much a man of his own age that it seems he himself was reluctant to come to the conclusions to which his clinical experience was leading him. It was not only the sentimental ladies who shied away from the revelations, exclaiming, 'Oh, not the pretty little babies!' It is part of the measure of Freud's achievement that we now almost unquestioningly accept the notion of infantile sexuality in some aspects. In this field, however, a general impression can be seriously misleading; we need to look closely at Freud's argument and recognize all the implications of his approach. In particular, we will see how he not only extended the understanding of sexual development into childhood but also widened the whole concept of sexuality. The word that he used in this connection was 'libido', defining it as 'that force by which the sexual instinct is represented in the mind'. He added that it was to be regarded as 'analogous to the force of hunger or the will to power and other such trends' (quoted Jones, Vol. II., p. 316).

In building his theory, Freud started with the clues given by the adult sexual behaviour. He made a distinction between the *sexual object,* that is to say the person from whom the sexual attraction comes, and the *sexual aim,* the act towards which the drive is directed. The normal sexual object is an adult of the opposite sex, but this is not always so: in cases of what Freud called 'inversion' a person of the same sex, or young children, may be the object of attraction. Equally, the aim of adult sexuality is full intercourse, but for some people the aim can be diverted to other forms of sex play or even simply the desire to see another person naked. These deviations are described as 'perversions'. So even adult sexuality has a wide variety of forms. How does the sexual drive find these deviant objects and aims?

The answer for Freud lay in the understanding of sexual development as a whole. This is what he set out to explore in the *Three Essays;* what he says there is, however, not his final conclusion, for he continued to modify his ideas throughout his life. Even the *Essays* themselves were substantially amended and expanded as they went through six editions in the course of twenty years. The main outlines of his thesis were, however, clear and he maintained them through all opposition.

The logical starting point of his theory is in the notion of libidinal energy. This, as a part of his instinctual equipment, is present in the human being from the start of life. Its biological function is to make pleasurable various activities which are necessary for the maintenance of life. So first of all it is attached to feeding. 'Sucking at the mother's breast is the starting point of the whole sexual life, the unmatched proto-type of every later sexual satisfaction.' (XVI. 314) The biological necessity for this first pleasurable process of feeding can be observed to be overlaid with the element of playful enjoyment for both a mother and her child. Freud was prepared to link this fact with the way that both breast and lips remain important areas of stimulation in adult sexuality, what he called 'erotogenous zones'. These are parts of the body which for adult sexuality still convey pleasurable sensations even though their functional side is now divorced from the overtly sexual. They remain, however, capable of becoming the centre of the libidinal focus if the person regresses to an earlier phase of satisfaction as will be described later.

While this link of oral pleasure to later sexuality is comparatively easy to accept, the next stage is apt to encounter considerably more resistance. For Freud was convinced that the developing infant moved from the oral phase to the anal phase of libidinal organization; his experience of satisfaction centred round his bowel movements. Not only were these capable of being pleasurable in themselves, but, at least in civilized society, they provided the infant with his first taste of power. He could exercise considerable control over his bodily functions, storing up the moment of pleasure and at the same time this provided a means of offering, or retaining something valuable or at least important to the anxious parents or nursemaids who concerned themselves with his toilet training. This stage of libidinal organization is subsequently subject to the severest repression and only emerges clearly in analysis.

The final stage of development is when the infant has discovered the area of genital pleasure and expresses this in masturbation. According to Freud there are two phases of masturbatory activity: that of early infancy and another at the highest point of infantile sexual development at about the age of four.

Here we can see that the stages of libidinal organization mark a shift in the sexual aim; oral stimulation gives place to anal and then to genital. The years of development are then followed by a 'latency period' in which sexuality is largely quiescent before coming into the foreground again at puberty. There remains the other question of the choice of a sexual object. Initially the mother is the obvious recipient of her child's affection and it was in working out the implications of this choice that Freud elaborated the notion of the Oedipus complex.

His theory was that the male infant, desiring his mother for himself, finds this wish frustrated by his father. The ensuing jealousy and hatred of his father conflict with his genuine love for his parents which is also present. Added to this sense of badness may be a fear for his father as the possible victim of the ill-wishes which are directed at him. (Freud seems to have discovered in his own analysis the guilty fear that his jealousy had 'murdered' his brother Julius.) Finally there is the recognition that the sexual feelings which he experiences are disapproved of by the external world. In the lengthy case history of Little Hans (*Complete Works X*) these theories, worked out from the analysis of adults, find remarkable corroboration from the unravelling of a phobia in a five-year-old boy.

While the Oedipus complex seems in practice to elucidate the family relationships of the small boy, it is not nearly so clear how the lines of sexuality develop for the girl child. At one point Freud explored the hypothesis that there was a parallel experience for her, with her father as the sexual object and her mother as the rival.

Perhaps because the situation in the case of the girl is necessarily complicated by the fact that the mother provides the initial physical experience for her just as much as for the boy, the theory has remained far more obscure and less plausible. So the contrast between the sexes does not achieve the stark polarity of the original Oedipus complex. On the other hand, Freud would have been quick to point out that this presentation has made one important over-simplification, in that every person has both a male and female make-up, although, of course, one or other side is bound to be dominant. It was in the light of this that he wrote that he was accustoming himself 'to the idea of regarding every sexual act as a process in which four persons are involved'.

In a rather similar way Freud produced a clear exposition of the Castration complex from the male point of view but was much less plausible when writing of the female experience. As he saw it, the small boy begins with an interest in his penis as part of his physical make up. It proves to be the source of comforting and forbidden sensations. His interest may then shift to discovering whether everyone else shares the same physical equipment. In the case of Little Hans, the child, aged four, had worked out that it was one of the distinguishing marks of animate as opposed to inanimate objects. Then comes the alarming discovery that the female has not got one and the conjecture that it may be that such a valuable possession can be removed. This, Freud suggested, can be reinforced by the unfortunate threats of even educated parents to 'cut it off' as a punitive response to discovering the child masturbating. His explanation of the female development and exploration of genital sensations is far less coherent or plausible and perhaps unconsciously reflects his socially conditioned view of women's place generally. One is tempted to hazard the guess that what Freud writes about the male development gains its greater authenticity from the fact that it is the fruit of his own self-analysis as well as clinical observation. For instance, the first mention of the Oedipus complex is in a letter to Fleiss dated October 15, 1897: 'One single thought of general value has been revealed to me. I have found in my own case too, falling in love with the mother and jealousy of the father, and I now regard it as a universal event of early childhood.'

As far as the choice of sexual object is concerned,

37

therefore, Freud taught that the first contact is with the mother, and ideally from this the developing personality is encouraged to establish the basis on which later good object relationships can be made with a member of the opposite sex. Where the initial experiment fails, the child will learn to look for alternatives, either in members of his or her own sex, or with children rather than adults, or even with substitutes for persons altogether.

Perversion and Permissiveness

Once it has been established how a person progresses to maturity in the choice of both sexual object and aim, it becomes easier to understand what happens when this natural development is thwarted. If we think of the three stages of libidinal organization as a kind of ascending ladder, then in later life where sexual expression is blocked altogether, there is a regression back to an earlier stage where the person found satisfaction. So there may be a move back from the genital orientation to the anal or the oral. If this is expressed directly it is seen as a sexual perversion. Equally a man failing in a heterosexual relationship may regress in his choice of a sexual object to another man or some other forms of inversion.

It may be, however, that there is a strong internal inhibition which prevents the person from acting out the sexual implications of the regressed desires. Then instead of regressed behaviour there will appear the symptoms of a neurotic illness. Hence Freud's dictum: 'Neuroses are the negative of perversions.'

From so bald a statement it might seem that the logic of the situation was to urge everyone to a free expression of their sexual desires and then no one would suffer from neurosis. This is just the sort of calumny that has

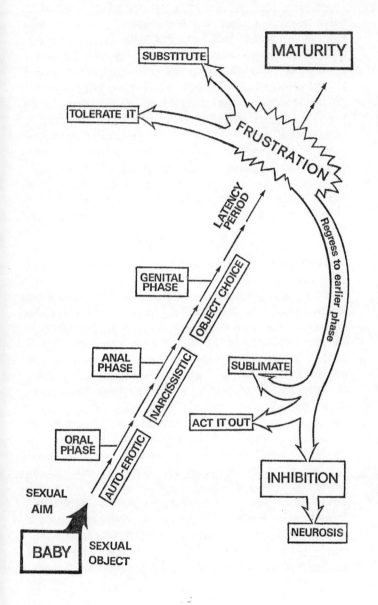

been levelled against the teaching of psycho-analysis precisely because its full statement of the situation has not been given proper attention. At the stage of the initial frustration in adult living Freud suggests that three alternatives are open to a person. They can either tolerate the frustration, or they can divert the libidinal energy into some more socially acceptable form; or, finally, failing these there is the way of regression to an earlier level. At the point of regression there is still the option of whether the perverse satisfaction shall be made conscious and brought under control or again whether some form of sublimation is possible. The whole process with its various options may be summarized in the accompanying diagram.

It is important to insist that to take a psycho-analytic point of view is not the same as advocating the most permissive of courses. When Freud first gave his *Five Lectures on Psycho-analysis* in the United States in 1909 the comment was made in a Canadian University, 'An ordinary reader would gather that Freud advocates free love, removal of all restraints and a relapse into savagery.' Although academic opinion is today likely to be better informed, there are still many 'folk-myths' in currency of sinister psychiatrists who advise innocent girls to sleep with their boy-friends or prescribe extra-marital affairs. Because Freud examined the basis of sexuality it did not make him into a wild libertarian. In a paper on *Civilized Sexual Morality and Modern Nervousness* he did put forward the view that current morality was putting an intolerable burden on people who were condemned to a marriage relationship that was all too often sexually unsatisfactory. The result was a double standard of morality, not officially recognized and working very much to the detriment of women. In the light of this, he declared himself in favour of revolutionary changes,

40

but these were all in the direction of greater mental health and not the urgings of someone in favour of moral anarchy.

It might be thought that Freud had pushed the barriers of information about the first experiences of the human infant as far as they could well go. What could be hidden in the unconscious mind prior to the most primitive relationship of the child with the mother? Freud was able to answer that at first the child is not capable of distinguishing 'the other' at all. It is aware of the world only as organized around itself. Therefore there is at first no 'object' for its first stirrings of sexuality. It has only sexual aims which it endeavours to fulfil through its own body. This period is, therefore, called the 'auto-erotic' phase. Subsequent to this and before the establishment of object-choice proper, Freud later came to add a stage to which he gave the name 'Narcissism'. This was a period when the child was aware of itself in its own right, in a sense beginning to be an individual but the object of its own sexual interest.

Freud tended to equate the period of auto-eroticism with the oral and early anal phase of sexual aim, the period of narcissism follows, and then, mid-way through the anal period there emerges 'consideration for the object'. It should be noted that Freud distinguishes between the process of object-choice and the emotion of love which he saw as being something reserved for the 'relation of the total ego to objects'. (XIV 137) What he meant by the 'total ego' we must consider in the next section.

To Love and to Work

'Freud was once asked what he thought a normal person should be able to do well. The questioner probably expected a complicated answer. But Freud, in the curt way of his old days, is reported to have said: "Lieben und arbeiten" (to love and to work). It pays to ponder on this simple formula; it gets deeper as you think about it. For when Freud said "love" he meant *genital* love and genital *love;* when he said love *and* work, he meant a general work-productiveness which would not preoccupy the individual to the extent that he loses his right or capacity to be a genital and loving being. Thus we may ponder, but we cannot improve on "the professor's" formula.' (Erik H. Erikson. *Childhood and Society,* p. 256)

The formula sounds simple enough. The psychiatrist's appointment book is filled with the names of people who cannot achieve it. In his research and writing Freud was concerned both to understand what happened to people that blocked their path to fulfilment and to learn to which kinds of them it was realistic to offer help. For he was to be very clear, at least toward the end of his life, that there were some forms of neurotic illness which it might be possible for a therapist to understand and yet be unable, at least through psycho-analysis, to heal.

We have already taken note of the beginnings of his understanding of the problem of hysteria. Within the field of the psychoneuroses there are also people who find their lives severely limited by anxiety. At times this will appear as an acute state which is totally incapacitating; at others it will be canalized into some specific fear or phobia, perhaps of open spaces, or of being shut in; or it can be focused down even more exactly to a fear of one kind of animal or one kind of situation. Other people suffer from the compulsion to some form of obsessional conduct, the fulfilling of a ritual without which life becomes unsafe. There are also severe experiences of depression, leaving a person without any sense of their own intrinsic worth or unable to find any joy or hope in living. Others become suspicious and ready to imagine enmity or criticism from all sorts of quarters and so find the open, easy paths of social contact are closed. Finally there are people who suffer from specific forms of sexual immaturity which hamper them in their ordinary enjoyment of living.

Within this wide variety of disability Freud felt that it was possible to make a distinction between two definite points where the personality had become distorted. One was at the level of development before relationships were formed with others, that is to say at the narcissistic level. Here the problem is within the structure of the personality, the person's relationship to himself is disorganized and produces the severe depressive illness, the paranoid delusions of persecution and all the phantasies that centre upon the self. Psycho-analysis can elucidate the path that led to the illness but is not equipped to offer help. The reason for this is that in the end the tool by which analytic therapy works is the transference. That is to say, analyst and patient are setting up a controlled situation in which the distorted relationship to the other can be experienced, examined and so changed. Such faulty relationships, Freud believed, went back to the attempt of the child to relate to his parents through the desires, fear and guilt which make up the Oedipus complex. The 'transference neuroses' were therefore those which arose out of the failure to work through that primitive situation. Sexual problems most often led straight back to the 'first love-affair'. The obsessional patient is someone striving to keep under control terrifying aggressive feelings, which get disguised and then controlled by 'prohibitions, renunciations and restrictions upon his freedom'. Anxiety, which could be traced back to the damming up of libidinal energy was also treatable

43

by analysis for here again within the transference the authority which seemed to deny the satisfaction could be understood and the conflict resolved.

For the validation of such formulations Freud would first of all point to the case histories of the successfully completed analyses of patients. But as he continued to work within this newly discovered world of the unconscious mind it became clear that there must be a model which gave coherence to his formulations. Almost a new geography of the mind needed to be drawn; if new words were to be used then their definition needed to be made clear.

The Id, the Ego and the Super-ego

First of all there was the notion of the Unconscious mind itself. It was clearly distinguished from the ordinary forms of consciousness. But there was also another set of material which, although not immediately present to consciousness, was capable of recall at will, which the unconscious material precisely was not. This too needed a name and was called the 'preconscious'. But then exactly what went to make up the Unconscious? At first it seemed to be simply a collection of repressed material. In the course of treatment, however, it became clear that the resistances were also unconscious, and so Freud was led to produce a new theoretical structure which appeared in 1922 in a work with the title, *The Ego and the Id*.

In this, he worked out a pattern of dynamic interaction within the psyche. Initially the new-born infant was simply a collection of instinctual drives whose overall aim was directed to decreasing the sensations of 'unpleasure'. This was a more complicated notion than simply 'getting comfortable', for Freud held that any sense of

44

excitation led to a sense of tension or unpleasure which needed to be discharged so that pleasure could be achieved with the reduction of tension. One cannot help feeling that his model here is drawn from the pattern of adult sexuality where the excitation is relieved in the discharge of the orgasm and a peaceful sense of completion is achieved. But this gives a rather forced sense to the 'unpleasure' which is being overcome.

This play of forces which make up the infant psyche comes into contact with the external world and out of this experience part of the id is brought to a new level of development as the ego. It is closely linked to the system of perception which makes contact with reality. As such there is a large part of the ego which is conscious of itself in the process of perception. On the basis of this contact, the ego endeavours to see that the needs of the id are harmonized and modified so that some measure of gratification is possible. 'In its relation to the id it is like a man on horseback, who has to hold in check the superior strength of the horse; with this difference, that the rider seeks to do so with his own strength while the ego uses borrowed forces' (that is to say the forces of reality as the ego perceives them). 'The illustration may be carried further. Often a rider if he is not to be parted from his horse is obliged to guide it where it wants to go; so in the same way the ego constantly carries into action the wishes of the id as if they were its own.'

As well as id and ego, Freud identified a third internal force, the super-ego. Succinctly described as 'the heir of the Oedipus complex' this is the part of the personality which lays down the law. While it might loosely be said that the idea represents what in common language is called conscience, the point of Freud's formulation is that it attempts to identify the source of that notion of 'oughtness' that each person has in varying degrees.

45

Partly it arises from the child's automatic identification with his parents. Added to this, in the course of the conflict of emotions which are engendered in the Oedipus complex the child internalizes or introjects his parents' value system because he has dealt with his problem of relationships by 'becoming' his father. A further dimension may be added if there is a feeling also that he 'must not be' his father, so that the process of identification will be in tension with a 'reaction-formation' against all that his father stands for. The result of these various pressures is the super-ego, part conscious, part unconscious, capable of being the source of terrible feelings of guilt and unworthiness.

This super-ego is also the means by which the mores of the race are handed on since the child in identifying with his parents links into their previous identification with a yet older generation.

Between the id and the super-ego, both making their demands, the ego strives to live in touch with the real world, and sometimes this can only be done by repressing demands from either side. The repressed super-ego can be the source of unconscious feelings of guilt which only emerge in the actions of a person who seems determined to court punishment.

As Freud examined the consequences of this new dynamic formulation of the inner world of the personality, there seems to be a need to pay more attention to the aggressive instincts which had been less exhaustively analysed than the sexual.

Anxiety and Aggression

In a work which was written in the period 1919–20, *Beyond the Pleasure Principle,* he had started on a curious new tack in which he refined the basic instincts within the psyche down to two. One was called Eros, which was the life-affirming principle, taking up the earlier ideas of libido as one of its components; over against this was the 'death instinct' which later acquired the name Thanatos. It seemed at first extremely implausible to suggest that the wish for death was an essential part of human existence. His argument began from the observation of a repetition compulsion in various people. Some of these were sufferers from war neuroses (the date was 1919) who repeated over and over again in their dreams the horrifying experiences which had led to breakdown. Equally he had watched his grandson, aged 19 months, playing a game of throwing away a cotton reel in imitation of the departure of his mother, an event which he disliked. Such behaviour linked in his mind with the pattern of some patients who tended to act out over and over again unpleasant experiences of their childhood.

He became convinced that some general law was at work in the things which he had observed and that the compulsion to repetition was really part of a pattern by which things returned to their beginning, so that in this sense the aim of life was a return to the peace and rest of unbirth or death. So at the heart of every human being he felt that he had discerned a process of destruction which he then used to account for the way that aggression gets turned out from the self into the external world. The normal interpretation is that there is an aggressive instinct that can become so inhibited that it is turned on to the self. Freud inverted the interpretation and saw externalized aggression as the defence against the death instinct. Extending this into the social field he asked whether war was not the nation's defence against internal strife and self-destruction. One cannot help feeling that the experience of the war years, especially in treating the

47

psychological casualties, may have influenced Freud's judgement in seeing things this way round.

It is again difficult with a brief summary to do justice to Freud's speculations in this direction. Baldly stated they are bound to seem extremely far-fetched, but perhaps the new understanding of the super-ego with its sometimes overwhelming burden of guilt made it possible to feel that there is within a person a destructive force which is not an outside invasion but part of his own make-up.

Quite apart from the theoretical arguments into which such speculations could lead, there is their use in the delineation of various patterns of character. If we accept Freud's premisses, what a man is depends to a great extent on the outcome of the three-cornered struggle between the id, the super-ego and the external world. The id we have seen is largely composed of the drives that are part of the human condition, but heredity may also play a part in varying the balance between specific components in the individual. How these find their satisfaction will depend on the way that a particular society is structured and on other criteria such as the financial position of the family, the historical circumstances, and everything else that goes to make up the reality which is perceived by the ego. Finally there is the super-ego to be satisfied, the internalized voice of authority.

The outcome of this may be that in one case a person may have a character which is marked by great acquisitiveness. Freud would trace this back to the anal stage when he first learned the pleasure and perhaps the power of saying 'What I have I keep'. Equally, the painter or sculptor may have taken the direction of their art initially from turning the fascination of playing with faeces into a socially acceptable path. Such a point of

48

view is not intended to reduce character traits to nothing but the primitive pre-genital drives and so devalue them. Rather the value of such an analysis lies in the understanding of how deep-seated are the differences between individuals. This might lead to a greater respect for each person's characteristic way of living and save us from attempts to impose uniformity. Doubtless sufficient social pressure can iron out difference but at considerable damage to the psychic structure of the individual. One can see why Freudian psychology is not acceptable within an ideology such as the Marxist which lays more stress upon social conformity than personal development.

Other patterns of character are built up, not by sublimating the drives, but by a reaction formation against them. So the house-proud mother, polishing her furniture and tidying her children, can be keeping at bay the otherwise overwhelming sense of her own 'dirtiness'. Equally, the exaggerated puritanism which makes a person something of a busybody, as a guardian of public morals, often seems to stem from the same need to deny their own badness. Such a way of dealing with the internal pressures is less satisfactory than a genuine sublimation because the element of denial absorbs considerable psychic energy, and socially the pattern tends to threaten the peace of mind of others. To sublimate a drive is to use its energy for a socially accepted end. In this way release is achieved creatively and what was unacceptable has been given a value which can be acknowledged. The reaction formation is a process of denial and just because of this seems often to include a kind of missionary drive. Where analytic insight can be achieved with such a person, the 'moral' overtones of their attitude can be understood in their true light and perhaps progress made to a genuine sublimation of the initial drive.

49

In such a discussion of the way in which human beings develop, it is clear that however detached a point of view the observer tries to adopt, as soon as there is any question of therapy, value judgements are introduced. We have, for instance, suggested above that sublimation is a 'better' way of dealing with pre-genital drives than reaction formation because the former leaves the person more free within himself. Once one has begun to evaluate the life-style of the individual on this basis, one is bound to bring the same criteria into play in considering institutions or whole societies. Such a development was very much in line with Freud's temperament; in the postscript to his *Autobiographical Study* he wrote: 'My interest after making a lifelong detour through the natural sciences, medicine and psychotherapy, returned to the cultural problems which had fascinated me long before, when I was a youth, scarcely old enough for thinking.'

His writing in this field began with *Totem and Taboo* (1912), *The Future of an Illusion* (1927), *Civilization and its Discontents* (1930) *and Moses and Monotheism* (1939). His concern was to show how the inner life of the individual was mirrored on a large scale in the history of societies. In particular, he focused his attention on religious practices, since he saw them as the counterpart in society of the personal rituals that the individual used for dealing with excessive pressure from the super-ego.

There is much that is acutely perceptive in what he has to say about these aspects of human behaviour, but it is generally agreed that these writings lack the scientific discipline that would make them serious contributions to the study of either religion or anthropology. Yet like so many intuitive works they offer suggestions that start interesting trains of thought. Although few would accept either the anthropological reconstruction of the origins of totemism or agree with the historical guesses about the origins of Moses, yet Freud's observation of the mechanisms at work in religious communities as he saw them is often clinically acute. With something of a blind prejudice he dismissed all religion as neurotic, and this was unfortunate because it made believers deaf to the valid criticism which he levelled against those practices which reinforced fears and guilt feelings and kept people dependent instead of assisting their growth into self-reliance and freedom. But to point out such failures in religious practice is not necessarily to remove the grounds of rational belief.

The acute perception of the psycho-analyst has much of value to contribute in a great many areas of our living provided we do not imagine him to speak with either the voice of God or of the Devil. We cannot set him up as the arbiter of what we ought to do or be, we cannot ask him to tell us about ultimate truth. Equally we must not fear that he can destroy our values or undermine a religious faith if it is a true one. By profession he observes and particularly takes note of the discrepancies between our protestations and our actions or our public and private selves. In calling attention to the contradictions that we had not noticed, he offers us the chance to bring our living into a more coherent pattern. At this level the thought and work of Freud have contributed to the possibility of a greater reality in living for people far outside the circle of those with whom a psychiatrist is professionally concerned.

3

SIGNIFICANCE

FREUD DIED on September 23, 1939, in a house in
London. He had been forced to escape from Vienna
in the previous year when it became apparent that even
his international distinction would not keep him safe
indefinitely from the anti-semitic persecution of the
Nazis.

His arrival in England brought notices of welcome
from the British medical press, evidence that he was now
an established figure throughout the psychiatric world.
His ideas had aroused violent hostility, and perhaps
naturally he had drawn about him a few devoted
adherents who formed the nucleus of what became the
International Psycho-analytic Association. In the difficult years he had felt a deep sense of isolation, and conse-
quently there were times when he made considerable
emotional demands on his followers, regarding any criticism or disagreement as disloyalty. The history of the
developing practice of analytical therapy shows a dis-
tressing number of heresy hunts; Jung and Adler are
the best known colleagues who found that it was not
possible to develop their own approach alongside Freud's.
Jung wrote later: 'Under the impress of Freud's personality I had, as far as possible, cast aside my own judgements and repressed my criticisms. That was the pre-

requisite for collaborating with him.' (C. J. Jung. *Memories, Dreams, Reflections.* p. 187)

Although it is clear that Freud could be fiercely defensive about a particular aspect of his work when it came under criticism, yet at the same time he was continually developing his theories. Psycho-analytic teaching was very different in 1939 from what it was in 1890. It is only to be expected that it should have gone on since his death.

There are perhaps two main reasons for the development. In the first place the spread of the ideas which were pioneered by Freud have to some extent altered the cultural environment. To this is due, at least in part, the fact that the pattern of neurosis has observably changed. Patients no longer tend to present the apparently isolated symptom which disrupts an otherwise socially adapted life; much more it is clear from the start that a neurosis is part of the personality. As a result the patient has found a new language in which to express his 'complaint'. Again, with the gradual acceptance of Freud's views on sexuality, it has become less difficult for the patient to express directly distress in that area of life.

Theoretically, development has also continued and this in two important directions. In the work of such analysts as Melanie Klein the inquiry has been taken back behind the oedipal stages and attention focused on the phantasy world of the child rather than any external events. Secondly, there has been a marked change in the use of models in thinking about the way the mind works. Freud was very much a product of the mechanist assumptions of the late nineteenth century. It is, therefore, not surprising that, when he looked round for a way of describing the libido, he turned to concepts of energy: as a result he talked in terms of quantities of excitation finding release. Later analytical thought has found it more helpful to start from the idea of a relationship to objects rather than the more mechanistic view. Such thinking is to be found particularly in the work of the British analysts, Winnicott and Fairbairn.

All this is to go beyond Freud's life and from the standpoint of 1939 to look into the future. Yet it is only as one does this that the greatness of his contribution to the whole culture becomes clear. He was not an infallible source of information about the human mind as some have mistakenly tried to claim, but he was a pioneer leading the way into a whole uncharted territory of research.

In the end, posterity is likely to remember Freud's genius which has helped a whole culture penetrate deeper into the world of mental illness, and at the same time to see itself more clearly. To achieve this took considerable courage to speak as he did in the face of angry prejudice. In recording his life, however, it is important not to forget the triumph of his own personal maturation. From the beginning there is plenty of evidence that Freud had a difficult personality, bearing the scars of both the interpersonal confusions and the social disadvantages of his first years. A jealous, demanding fiancé, a touchy colleague, he ended his life full of serenity, although the last period brought a very severe test. For he had suffered from a cancer of the mouth which in the years 1923 to 1939 necessitated thirty-three operations and occasioned him considerable pain. His ability to persevere through this, both in writing and in the painstaking work of therapy, is perhaps in part a tribute to the work of self-investigation that he had undertaken in his own analysis.

Through the eighty-three years of his life his mind and vision had ranged wide. He had opened new areas of understanding to the whole of our culture and his personality had grown to match this achievement. It is perhaps significant that his devoted friend and disciple, Ernest Jones, could find only the language of poetry and religion to express his feelings at the Funeral Oration:

'His creative spirit was so strong that he infused himself into others. If ever man can be said to have conquered death itself, to live on in spite of the King of Terrors, who held no terror for him, that man was Freud.

'And so we take leave of a man whose like we shall not know again. From our hearts we thank him for having lived; for having done; and for having loved.'

He deserves the admiration of all of us who live in the light of the discoveries that are uniquely his.

SHORT READING LIST

Books by Freud

FREUD, *The Interpretation of Dreams,* Allen and Unwin.
  Two Short Accounts of Psycho-Analysis, Pelican Books.
  New Introductory Lectures in Psycho-Analysis, Allen
  and Unwin.

These are the works by Freud which form the best
introduction to his writings. As well as appearing in the
above form these titles form part of his *Complete Psychological Works,* published in twenty-three volumes by the
Hogarth Press.

Books about Freud

ERNEST JONES, *Sigmund Freud, Life and Work,* 3
  Volumes, Hogarth Press 1953–59.

DAVID STAFFORD-CLARK, *What Freud Really Said,*
  Pelican Books 1967.

J. A. C. BROWN, *Freud and the Post-Freudians,* Pelican
  Books 1961.

ERICH FROMM, *Sigmund Freud's Mission,* Allen and
  Unwin 1959.

R. S. LEE, *Freud and Christianity,* J. Clarke 1948.

Books about developing thought in psycho-analysis

D. W. WINNICOTT, *The Child, the Family and the Outside World,* Pelican Books 1964.

JOHN BOWLBY, *Attachment and Loss,* Hogarth Press
  1969, Pelican Books 1971.